Elevator Versus Bus

Public Transit Ideas

Bryan Costales

Fool Church Media

Published by

Fool Church Media
Eugene, Oregon

This book is a work of opinion. Names, places and incidents either are the product of the author's imagination or are used fictitiously. Other than well known historical people or events, any resemblance to actual persons, living or dead, events or locales is entirely coincidental.

Elevator Versus Bus

1st Edition 2021: Fool Church Media
Cover Art by Bryan Costales

Amazon Softcover ISBN: 978-1-945232-41-1
Kindle ISBN: 978-1-945232-40-4

Manufactured/Printed in the United States of America

Table Of Contents

To

Bus Riders everywhere!

Acknowledgments

I thank all those that have commented on my blog,"Munifest Destiny." I also thank the folks at nexdoor.com, who filled out the occasional survey, and the people with LTD and MUNI, who have answered all my many emailed questions.

I finally thank my wife Terry for her copy edits and constant support, and George Jansen for his insightful feedback and thoughtful critique.

Part 1

Overview

"You live your life at the time
you live it—you don't have
much of an overview when
what's happening to you is
still happening."

—John Irving, *In One Person*

1

Mission Statement

The Lane County (Oregon) Transit District's public Mission Statement is the following text from their website:

> "We are honored to serve a diverse community of commuters, students, seniors, and families on our buses everyday."

The above mission statement is typical of many small town transit districts. It references buses, and lists particular users. Many transit districts are similar: neither inspiring nor leading logically or emotionally to better public transit. The main problem is that they describe what they presently do, but do not describe what might be desirable and possible.

But suppose a mission statement similar to the following was used instead:

> "We shall provide a fast, comfortable, convenient, safe service that will, over the next 25 years, attract progressively more privately owned motor vehicle drivers, get them off the road, and thereby reduce the

district's carbon footprint and improve the flow of remaining traffic."

This latter sort of mission statement implies the district intends to change automobile drivers into public transit riders. As you will learn throughout this chapter, such a concept is a reasonable one.

Attract Drivers

Imagine the previous improved mission statement and ask: What qualities a public transit system must possess in order to attract drivers?

1. Public transit must appear to be visibly faster than cars and ideally, appear to be much faster.

2. Public transit must arrive at any given stop or station no less frequently than once every ten to fifteen minutes.

3. Like an elevator, public transit should always run. However, it may need to run less frequently after midnight through before dawn. But it should never cease running.

4. A public transit ride should cost significantly less than driving between the same locations (despite the fact that the cost of driving is well hidden and government subsidized).

5. No residence or business should be farther than 200 yards from a bus or train stop. Any further and people will be less likely to use public transit.

6. Public transit should be based on a grid design, rather than a hub design. A grid design is more immune to outages. The Grid design is more likely to provide a connection between any two arbitrary horizontal or vertical locations.

7. Public transit vehicles must be sanitary, clean, climate controlled, well lit, comfortable, and safer than driving.

First we explore the cost of such possible systems, and after that we explore the meaning of each of the above numbered points.

Public Transit Cost

An improved mission statement has as its goal to, "Attract progressively more privately owned motor vehicle drivers." This goal requires fast frequent public transportation that only shuts down for routine maintenance. Fast, frequent public transport is more expensive to build and operate than is slow, infrequent public transit which routinely shuts down at night and that doesn't run on holidays.

Good public transit costs more than bad public transit. Below, we show how much more—not in dollar amounts, but rather in relative ratios.

A **diesel bus** route usually has bus stops that are easily moved, and cheap to build. This is the most common form of public transit, found in most small towns. A bus carries the fewer riders than all other forms of public transit. Each bus requires a driver, which incurs a labor cost. Because bus stops are minimal and not fixed, there is little motivation for investors to build new housing or businesses near such temporary bus stops.

Electric bus routes are twice as expensive to build as diesel bus routes. They require either overhead wires for power, or in-street recharging areas at layover bus stops to recharge batteries. Electric buses carry the same number of passengers and drivers as diesel buses. Because bus stops are not fixed, there is little motivation to build new housing nor to locate businesses near such temporary bus stops.

Bus Rapid Transit (BRT) routes are twice as expensive as electric bus routes to construct and operate. BRT generally runs more frequently than regular buses and has semi-permanent bus stops that resemble stations. BRT, for example, needs concrete slabs at stations with embedded wires to guide the bus to a close stop for level boarding. BRT is the minimum level of service that can allow bicycles on board. BRT carries 35% more passengers than regular buses, yet each bus requires a driver. Because BRT stations are semi-permanent, construction of new residences or businesses near stops makes only a little bit more sense.

Light Rail (LR) is twice as expensive to build as BRT. LR requires tracks embedded in the street and overhead wires to power the trains (although some light rail uses a third power rail imbedded in the street). Their stations are no more expensive than BRT stations to construct, although longer stations may be required to accommodate multi-car trains. LR carries two to eight times more passengers than do buses,

10

because LR can be assembled into multi-car trains (note that buses cannot be connected together to form bus trains). Multi-car trains only require a single driver which reduces labor costs. Light Rail, when it shares the road, is called a Trolley. Light Rail when it is separated from the road (grade separated), is called a train. Because tracks are much harder to move, Light Rail stations *strongly* encourage new multi-use construction around them.

Subway Light Rail is twice as expensive to build as surface LR. Subways are either built using the trench and fill method, or bored with a tunneling machine. Stations are underground with above ground sidewalk access. Subways do not interact with cars at all. Subways are the best bet at attracting automobile drivers onto public transportation. Subway stations, once built, are rarely if ever moved. New mixed-use construction near such stations is a certainty.

Inter-city Rail is twice as expensive to build as Subway. Inter-city rail is generally powered by overhead wires. It can reach medium speeds of 75 to 125 miles per hour between city stops. It must never share the road with automobiles and bridge over or tunnel under all grade crossings and waterways. Inter-city Rail requires state government involvement.

High Speed Rail (HSR) is from two to ten times more expensive to build as Inter-city Rail. HSR would only be used to connect major cities such as Seattle to Portland, or San Francisco to Los Angeles, or Dallas to Houston.

Amortization

Another cost item to consider is that buses have to be replaced once every eight to ten years of operational use. That is the longest interval that tax laws allow buses to be amortized.

Roads need to be resurfaced at similar intervals. More often if they are being dug up for new utilities upkeep, changes, or additions.

When comparing modes of transport, consider:

- A bus will typically have to be replaced five times over the life of a rail car. But since a light rail car holds twice as many passengers as a bus, two buses will be replaced five times (or one bus ten times) over the life of a light rail car. A bus costs a half million, a light rail car costs $2.5 million each. That means $5 million is spent on a bus over the life of a $2.5 million dollar light rail car.

- Roads are typically resurfaced ten times during the life of rails. Even though rails appear to be imbedded in asphalt, they are actually set in a concrete slab underneath, with asphalt set on top. So resurfacing neither effects the tracks nor the underlying concrete.

What The Driver Sees

If a mission statement has the goal of attracting drivers, one needs to understand the perception of those automobile drivers.

When a automobile passes a bus that is pulled over to pick up passengers, that car's driver will likely believe that driving is far faster than riding the bus. After all, his/her private automobile never needs to stop to pick up random passengers.

When an automobile slows to let a bus pull back into traffic, that driver will certainly resent the way the bus slows traffic.

When an automobile driver walks to his/her car and sees a bus pass, that driver might think, "I am glad I don't have to rub elbows with the great unwashed."

This perception is a problem caused by the nature of buses. It is shared by all local transit, including Bus Rapid Transit and Streetcars. All three share the roads with motor vehicles and all three cause drivers to believe that driving is faster and more convenient than taking public transit.

For public transit to actually be faster than driving, public transit must not share the road. The solution to this problem is either to create new roads exclusively designed for buses, or locate public transit over or under roads.

When drivers begin to ride public transit, the characterization of bus riders will transform from one of regular (unwashed) folks, into one of (clean) automobile drivers as passengers.

Qualities To Attract Drivers

An improved mission statement strives to attract drivers as passengers. For that to happen, public transit must appear faster, more convenient, safer. and more comfortable than driving. In general light rail and inter-city trains are significantly faster than buses mixed with traffic. Their high speed is made possible by grade separation from traffic (as well as separation from bicycles and pedestrians). Often rail can easily reach speeds of 70 to 100 miles per hour between stops. Rail is most efficient when electrified.

Imagine that rail can take you to your destination two, or three time faster, than driving. Wouldn't this encourage abandonment of more cars than a bus that will always discourage car abandonment?

1. Public transit must appear to be visibly faster than cars and ideally, appear to be much faster.

Only public transit that does not share the road with buses or cars can provide such a contrast. Imaging driving when a bus pulls out in front of you, yes you can pull into the other lane and pass the bus, but you will never believe that any bus is faster than driving.

Now imagine planning to meet a friend at the movies. You endured bumper-to-bumper, day-end commuter traffic, and then you must search a crowded parking lot before finding an open parking place. You found your friend already waiting at the box office. You asked, "How'd you get here so fast?"

He/She smiled and said, "I took the new subway. It was amazingly fast and comfortable. And I caught up with email on the ride."

2. Public transit must arrive at any given stop or station no less frequently than once every ten to fifteen minutes.

Many a bus rider has gotten to a bus stop just after the bus has passed. When the bus runs hourly, or even every half hour, such a missed bus causes the rider to wait for an hour or a half hour for the next bus. Not only is this frustrating in the extreme, it can also discourage the rider from ever riding a bus again. Twenty minutes is at the very edge of tolerable in good weather. Ten and fifteen minutes are correspondingly more and less tolerable in all types of weather.

The ideal frequency of public transit should be once per ten minutes during the prime hours of 6:00 a.m. to 9:00 p.m. One solution is to run buses on shorter routes. If a shorter route takes twenty minutes to traverse (including a driver break between runs) then four buses would allow buses to pass each stop once per ten minutes.

Well designed public transit will allow a rider to miss a bus or train without harm, in the knowledge that another bus or train will arrive soon.

> 3. Like an elevator, public transit should always run. However, it may need to run less frequently after midnight through before dawn. But it should never cease running.

Recall last New Year's Eve. Traditionally, new year's eve is the time of year for the police to arrest drunk drivers. Why should anyone drive drunk? After all we have taxi's, ride share, and designated drivers. But is that enough? Isn't it better to run transit at all times so nobody ever needs to drive drunk, stoned, tired or otherwise impaired?

If buses are to replace cars, shouldn't buses run at all times every day? Perhaps at least once per hour from midnight to 6:00 a.m. San Francisco runs "owl" service hourly during those times on major routes. Portland stops running between midnight and 3:30 a.m., and then only starts running selected longer routes after 4:00 a.m. New York's MTA runs reduced service between 1 a.m and 5 a.m. Eugene, Oregon shuts down between midnight and 6:00 a.m.

A person will only ride a form of transportation if that transportation is reliable. One would no more rely on a car that breaks down every night, than on a bus system that ceases running at the wrong time every night. Would you move into a building where the elevators only worked from 6 a.m. to midnight? Of if an elevator wouldn't run on holidays? If you wouldn't move into such a building, why do you continue to live in a town where public transit shuts down at arbitrary times?

> 4.   A public transit ride should cost significantly less than driving between the same locations (despite the fact that the cost of driving is well hidden and government subsidized).

When one considers the cost of public transit, one rarely contrasts that cost to the actual cost of driving.

Most drivers consider driving free, or at worst just the cost of gas. Few drivers ever include all the costs of driving in their computations.

- Cars are often financed over time with a loan. Those loan payments are a part of a car's monthly cost. The interest on a loan should also be part of a car's monthly cost.

- All cars depreciate (lose value) over time. New cars depreciate the moment they are driven off the lot. So this often hidden loss of value should also be counted as a cost of driving.

- Gas, of course, is more expensive if you drive long distances, or if you drive a gas-guzzling SUV or pickup. Gas is also a cost of driving.

- Annual registration is another expense. In some states the cost is based on the depreciated value of your car. Other states charge annually for miles driven.

- The cost of car insurance is a major expense. The cost varies based on your driving record, the nature of your coverage, and how long you've been insured with the current company.

It can range from a few hundred dollars annually to over thousands of dollars annually.

- The cost of occasional repairs and the cost of tires are often overlooked. Routine shop work typically averages a thousand dollars a visit. A blown transmission or engine can cost much more. Tires last about five years of average driving and cost a few hundred dollars to replace.

- The cost of parking meters, and the cost of parking tickets should also be considered as a cost of driving.

- The cost of your private parking garage. This is either calculated into your mortgage, or as part of Home Owners Association dues in the instance of a condominium or townhouse.

The last time we computed our car's cost, it ended up costing $1,000 per month despite the fact we rarely drove it.

Compare that to the cost of a monthly transit pass, between $50 and $120 per month ($600 to $1400 per year) depending on the transportation district. In the case of Eugene, Oregon's LTD, the cost is zero for people over 55 years old. In the case of San Francisco's MUNI the cost is zero for local residents over 65 years old.

It is not enough for public transit to say how cheap it is, it must instead stress how expensive it is to drive. One way to encourage drivers to ride public transit is to charge more for parking. A well run transit district should both administer parking and should derive operating funds from the enforcement of parking.

5. No residence or business should be farther than 200 yards from a bus or train stop. Any further and

people will be less likely to use
public transit.

As a rule of thumb, no home or business should be further from a transit stop then 600 feet (the length of two American football fields). That distance is about the furthest that any reasonable person is willing to walk in order to catch public transit.

A well designed transit district would lay a grid over a map and compute the location of transit stops to reduce the walking distance between stops.

A problem with suburban neighborhoods is that they are laid out to minimize internal traffic, with few connections to the surrounding grid, and with many internal cul de sacs. Such suburban neighborhoods are less amenable to nearby bus connections unless a convoluted route is created.

The disabled, new mothers, and elderly are least likely to walk a long way to a transit stop. Such people that need help should have access to smaller on-call transit to take them to regular transit stops or, even better, to their destinations.

6.   Public transit should be based on a grid design, rather than a hub design. A grid design is more immune to outages. The Grid design is more likely to provide a connection between any two arbitrary horizontal or vertical locations.

Imagine going to a movie. Consider a trip taking public transit downtown to a hub, and then back out from the hub to the movies. Wouldn't it be better to take public transit directly to the movies and skip the hub?

The hub design always requires the rider to travel downtown to a hub and then out again from that hub.

The grid design is vastly more amenable for direct trips.

A grid design will also place transit stops closer to where people live and work. Imagine traveling downtown and then back out again to the airport. Wouldn't it be better to only travel a quarter way toward the hub, then transfer to a direct horizontal route directly to the airport?

> 7.   Public transit vehicles must be
>   sanitary, clean, climate
>   controlled, well lit, comfortable,
>   and safer than driving.

Public transit should always be more comfortable than driving. That doesn't merely mean comfortable seats.

A bus ride causes passenger to be bounced around and jostled by every defect in the road's surface, from ripples in asphalt to pot holes. Contrast that to a ride on light rail, aside from an occasional mild sway, light rail rides are by contrast always very smooth.

> Conclusion: a bus ride is bumpy, whereas
> a light rail ride is smooth.

A bus ride generates a roar from the engine and from tires on the road surface. This make bus rides noisy, which inhibits introspection. Contrast that to light rail which is much more quiet, has only a mild squeal on corners, and a light clank sound when crossing a rail switch.

Conclusion: a bus ride is noisy, whereas a light rail ride is quiet.

A bus ride and light rail are equally susceptible to graffiti, loud music, litter, aggressive behavior and the smell of dropped or rotten food. This implies that all public transit should be routinely and thoroughly cleaned and disinfected.

Conclusion: bus and light rail can be equally dirty.

This also implies that fare inspectors be augmented or replaced by uniformed security personnel to keep riders safe.

Conclusion: bus and light rail can be equally unsafe.

So the bottom line is that light rail attracts more drivers, and is quieter and smoother than any bus. But all forms of transit are equally subject to dirt and crime.

Advertising And Promotion

For expensive public transit to succeed, it needs to be promoted and advertised.

1.   Develop and publish a revised mission statement with the goal of attracting automobile drivers.

2.   Develop and publish a twenty-five or fifty year plan.

3.   And then sell that mission and long term plan to the public with

powerful advertising and with a
suitable professional promotion
company.

The sensible transit district that transforms itself into a modern attractive pull to drivers, will need to transform its image. It will also have to lobby the state to get funds for its transformation. It will be reborn, Phenix-like, into a twenty-first century public transportation district, and a magnet for motor vehicle drivers.

Part 2

Funding Public Transit

"It is much easier to put existing resources to better use,
than to develop resources
where they do not exist."

—George Soros

2

$20 Fare By 2030

A scant one-hundred years ago, in the early 1900's, an adult bus-ride fare cost a mere nickel? That's right only five cents.

Currently, a adult fare on most buses costs $2 to $3 depending on the transit district. So how did we land in the current overpriced mess? How did the cost of public transportation rise so disturbingly fast?

There are four situations that effect the cost of riding public transit.

1. Inside car-centric towns, people would rather improve roads than subsidize public transit.

2. Fiscally conservative people prefer that the riding public pay, through fares, 100% of the cost of public transit.

3. There are federal grants to construct bus stops and to buy buses. But there are no federal grants for running or maintaining the system.

4. The generally held wrongful belief that only the poor, unwashed and elderly need public transit.

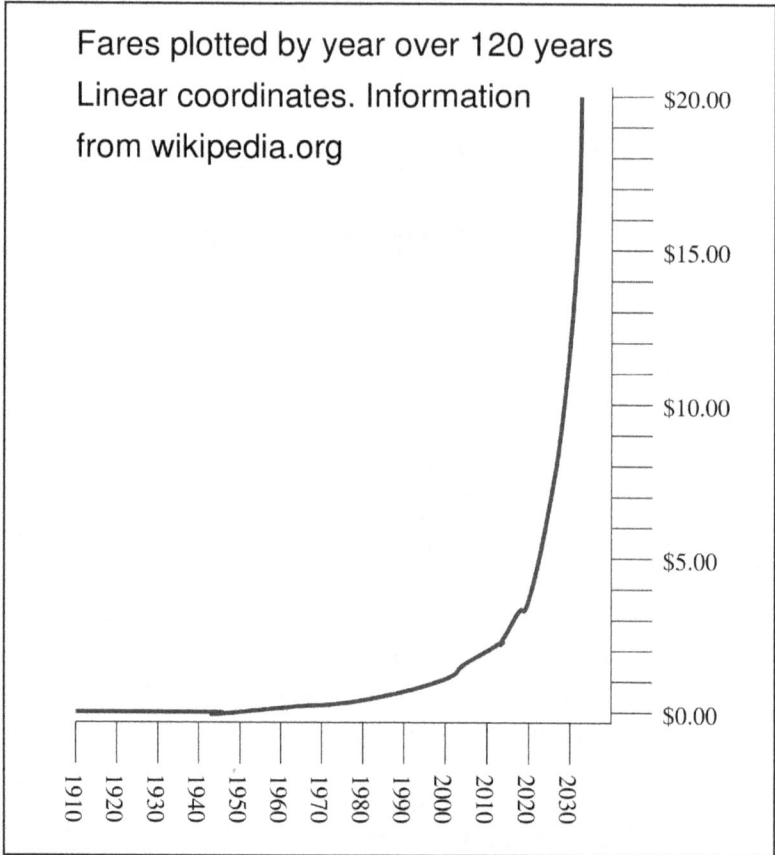

Fares plotted by year over 120 years
Linear coordinates. Information
from wikipedia.org

Figure 1.

To understand how we arrived at this situation, examine the above Figure1, It was based on publicly available data from Wikipedia.

Notice that a ride that started at a nickel in 1910, became a half-dollar in 1980, a dollar in 1992, and two-dollars in 2009.

Notice that the shape of the curve looks a lot like the curve of such things as inflation or anything else that increases faster over time, like payday loans.

In other words, everything costs progressively more over time. The line showing that growth also grows steeper over time (more vertical to the right). If the past is any indicator of the future (which it usually is), a typical bus fare will reach $20.00 by 2030. And fares will continue to rise exponentially (or perhaps hyperbolically) after that.

Until we bite the bullet and come up with an overriding counter-philosophy, fares will continue to rise at an exponential rate—rapidly pricing the poor and then the middle classes out of reach. In fact by 2050 only the rich will be able to afford public transit.

Questions To Ask

Consider the following three questions:

1. Should public transit be
    permanently free for all to ride?

If so, what would be the best tax source to support such a change? How much money would be saved by eliminating the machinery which collects the money, and by eliminating the cost of fare enforcement?

2. Should the cost of a bus ride be
    permanently pegged to some year
    in the past?

If so, which year and why? Is there any rational reason for selecting say $1.00 or $2.00 and making that permanent, versus selecting $0.00 and making that permanent?

3. Should fares increase by a fixed amount every year? Not by a fixed percentage.

If so, by what amount and how should that amount be determined? Should it be a nickel a year? Or a quarter once every five years?

Arguments over fare hikes and service cuts have no point unless we can settle on a single agreed philosophy about how much public transit should cost the riding passenger.

Politics

Conservatives argue that the riding public should pay the full cost of all public transit. But those same conservatives fail to advocate that drivers pay the full cost of all roads, bridges, and emergency services. Although public transit fares have increased dramatically since 1993, the federal gas tax has not increased at all (by even one penny) since 1993.

Liberals argue that public transit should be a right, and as such must be subsidized. But liberals fall short when called upon to increase capital expense or to move public transit off the roadways. Thus liberals favor some token fare, and favor keeping public transit inefficient.

Progressives believe that public transit is a right, and so should be free for all. They also believe that public transit has more right to the road than do automobiles. Progressives would gladly tax more to separate transit from cars, either putting one or the other over or under ground.

Whatever your political persuasion, you must agree that continued exponential growth in public transit fares is an unmaintainable situation that may lead to a future where nobody can afford to ride. In its place, automobiles (owned and/or shared) will again become the default mode of transportation, leading to more and more crowded roads and increased traffic and pedestrian deaths.

The cost of riding public transit is growing so fast, that the time to solve the problem becomes increasingly urgent. We had better solve this problem soon before it becomes impossible to solve.

Studies

City Lab studied the monthly passes offered by New York City's MTA. They found that, when the cost of monthly passes were tied to income (cheaper when poorer), all decreased monthly pass prices led to increased ridership with no increase in operational overhead.*

The Cache Valley Transit Department (in Logan, Utah) ran a study of all the transit districts in the United States that ran free public transit†. They concluded that free public transit was possible and could be successful, if any district had the "political will" to pull it off.

---

*. https://www.citylab.com/transportation/2019/03/
   nyc-subway-fare-bus-pass-price-mta-metrocard-public-
   transit/584836/

†. https://cvtdbus.org/wp-content/uploads/2018/09/
   2012-07-TCRP-fare-free-report.pdf

3

Residential Parking

Established in 1976, residential parking in San Francisco, was created to "preserve neighborhood-living within a major urban center." Residential parking is set up by area within the city, with each area designated by color and a one or two letter combinations.

Residential parking is indicated and regulated using signs. In area B, for example, a typical sign states that all parking is limited to two hours. But a resident with a current B decal may park all day without limit.

That is, any tourist visitor who can find a free parking place in such areas, may park for free for up to two hours, and after that will receive a ticket.

For example, a resident in area Y (South Beach of San Francisco) can purchase a permit ($110/year) from the city to park for free within that area. The exceptions are no parking during street cleaning and no car may remain parked without moving it for a maximum of three days. Other than those two limitations, a resident is allowed unlimited free parking for roughly 30 cents per day.

But why should the tourist visitor be allowed to park for free for two hours?

A better approach for regulating residential parking is through the use of metered parking. Instead of limiting parking to two free hours with signs, simply install parking meters and charge the going rate for parking.

A resident with a parking permit that matched the sign on a meter should be allowed to park at that meter for free. That is, a small sign or decal on the meter would replace the larger sign on the sidewalk.

Just as with parking as currently governed by signs, metered parking for visitors should also be limited to two hours.

An informal survey of a block near my home found two cars with the proper area decals and seven cars with no decals. If the block had been metered, seven cars would have generated income for the city. If the this area had been metered, the resident with a decal could still park for free.

Most cities will not copy the San Francisco method of residential parking. But whenever free parking is available, the access and reason for that free parking must be evaluated. Perhaps New York or Los Angeles, or Chicago handle parking differently. If so, then their systems should be examined. Are they really giving away too much free parking?

Because free parking is so central to driving, we delve deeper into this topic in the next chapter.

4

Should Parking Be Free?

An Imaginary Exercise

Imagine you will drive to Safeway (or Albertsons or Cosco or Wallmart) to pick up just a quart of milk for the this morning's breakfast or coffee, or just a dozen eggs. There are at least three good reason to drive in such situations:

1. The store is too far away or the route to it is too unsafe to walk, or too unsafe to bicycle.

2. The drive is easy and the parking is plentiful and free.

3. The bus or trolley doesn't exist or doesn't run frequently enough to take.

Now imagine you don't mind parking at a parking meter. That is, if there is sufficient time available and the cost is nominal.

1. Would you look for a meter with time already on it?

2. Would you hate meters because
   the cost of a ticket is too high?

We recognize that there are other common ways you already pay for parking. In large parking structures, you sometime take a token when you drive in and pay based on the time parked when you drive out. And, at some special events, you pay a flat fee when you first park and pay nothing more when you exit.

Next imagine you are about to drive to pick up those eggs. But this time you know ahead of time that the parking at the grocery store is not free. If the charge were 10 cents to park, you might become incensed that you have to pay anything at all to park. But, if the cost is lower (say 5 cents) would you mind paying that 5 cents to pick up eggs?

So the question for this exercise is: How much is fair to charge for parking to discourage frivolous driving? If you needed just eggs, you might do without those eggs rather than pay 50 cents, or one dollar, or five dollars to park? What is the correct amount?

Before we continue with this exercise, recall that new parking meters are "smart". Which means:

1. Smart meters can change the rate
   they charge based on parking
   demand. That is, the cost per
   minute would vary based on the
   time of day and a typical crowd of
   drivers.

2. Smart meters can be paid with
   charge cards or special discount
   cards for the disabled or poor.

3. Smart meters can automatically increase the cost per minute the longer you stay parked.

4. Smart meters can be remotely paid on your behalf by a supermarket or other business.

5. Smart meters can be looked up on a website or via a phone app to see if any parking is available.

Now imagine you are about to drive to buy eggs. But before you drive you bring up the store's website and notice that the lot is full or that parking is at its most expensive. Would you still make the trip?

But what if the store's website showed the lot was half-full and parking was $1.00 per hour. Would you drive there figuring you'd only need to park for 15 minutes. What if the cost were $2.00 per hour? $5.00 per hour? What if the website allowed you to reserve a parking space at a given time for a given number of minutes? Would you pay more for that ability?

Why Are We Doing This Exercise?

Before you ask that, consider once again the three reasons to drive:

1. The store is too far away or the route to it is too unsafe to walk, or too unsafe to bicycle.

This will be the case in low density areas, such as suburbs. rather than in a city's core. In cities, stores are most often within easy access to many who don't need to drive. In Suburbs, a grocery store can be four or five miles away. Much too far to walk, and almost too far to ride a bike.

2. The drive is easy and the parking is plentiful and free.

Note that parking must also be free. That cost is critical to understanding why people drive so much to shop. Yet we all have all driven to a store just before a holiday or before some event or after some disaster and had been unable to park because the parking lot was full of other cars prowling to find a space. So *sufficient* free parking is also necessary.

3. The bus or trolley doesn't exist or doesn't run frequently enough to take.

The lack of a bus, or access to only low frequency buses, is most often caused by lack of funds. If parking fees were not used to improve parks and not used to build new schools, but were instead used to improve public transit—then parking fees could help to solve this latter problem.

How Can Parking Meters Help?

If a suburban area had 100 stores and those stores averaged 50 parking spaces each and if each space charged an average of 10 cents per hour and each space were only occupied 4 hours per day on average, then that would create $60,000 a month for public transit. Now consider that a small town may have only 100 stores, whereas a medium sized town might have 500 stores. That would create $600,000 per month for public transit. And, if the rate were $1.00 instead of 10 cents, that $1.00 would create $6 million per month for public transit.

Now to be fair, it would not help to meter private parking, if parking on neighboring streets were free. If parking lots were not free and surrounding street parking was free, the average driver would look for street parking. Whenever shopping, searching residential streets for free parking along with other cars would frustrated drivers. Frustration would create risk to children, bicyclists, and the elderly.

So you would have to put smart meters on streets bordering stores. Perhaps for a few blocks outward from each store.

But why stop there? Why should parking anywhere be free?

When you park in your own garage or driveway that seems free, but it is not. Your driveway and garage are not free because its cost is computed into your mortgage, Home Owners Association Dues, rent, or property taxes.

Consider how parking meters could regulate all on-street and business parking:

1. Should it be cheaper to park, the nearer a parking meter is to a transit stop?

2. Should parking be more expensive the closer it is to an on-demand location like a store, or tavern, or theater?

3. Should the disabled always be given free parking, or just discounted parking?

4. Should the poor be given discounted parking or perhaps

free parking for special circumstances?

5. Should fire, police and ambulances park for free anywhere they need, when in service?

6. Should city officials (the mayor perhaps) park for free or be required to pay like everyone else?

7. Should street fairs have to reserve and pay for all the parking revenue that would be lost to close a street?

8. Should public off-street parking also have parking meters, such as parks, beach parking, and city owned parking lots?

9. Should church parking lots be free? Should all not-for-profit business parking lots be free?

10. Should state and county owned roads be exempt?

11. Should it be a crime to over park? Or should over parking be just a civil matter? Perhaps a mixture of the two? A civil matter until it becomes habitual?

12. Should the city issue parking cards? Smart cards for use in

smart meters, that you can refill online? Should those smart cards also be good on public transit?

13. Should coin meters be used because they cost a fourth as much as smart meters? But, on the down side, their hourly rate must be manually reset, making them much less attractive for intelligently designed parking.

14. Transit buses at bus stops should stop for free, but should other third-party or school buses pay for using those same stops?

15. Should there be free taxi-zones, or free Uber or Lyft or other shared ride zones? Should they, or should they not, be allowed cheaper parking?

As you can see, installing universal parking meters is not something to be taken lightly. It contains within it the promise of lots of money for improved frequent, convenient public transit, thereby removing more drivers from the roads. And, for those who need to drive, the roads will become less crowded. Also when people switch to buses, the demand for parking may drop and perhaps the cost of parking will also drop.

5

Accidental Benefits

A bus or a trolley can be involved in an accident. The fault may lie with the transit operator or with another vehicle operator. No matter who is at fault, public passengers are also harmed. Even if there is no physical harm, at a minimum the passengers will be delayed. Such delays can be anywhere from a few minutes to over many hours.

The other day, for example, a San Francisco MUNI express bus picked up passengers on Mission near Spear Street. A large truck pulled past the bus just close enough to clip the side mirror of the bus and twist it way off kilter. The truck driver pulled over and checked his own mirror before walking back to talk to the bus driver. In this instance the side mirror had not been broken, just miss aimed. The MUNI driver quickly corrected it. No supervisor needed to be called. The delay to the passengers was perhaps five minutes.

But what if the accident had been serious enough to call a supervisor? What if a bumper had been crumpled, or a window broken, or a mirror snapped off. The delay to the passenger could have been as long as an hour or more.

When another vehicle strikes a bus, or recklessly causes a trolley or bus to strike it, the driver is at fault and the driver's insurance card must be presented to a transit supervisor.

But imagine a different scenario. What if the law were changed to make the offending driver libel to both the transit company and individually to each of the passengers?

If a passenger could claim harm against the offending driver and that driver's insurance, instead of simply losing an hour, the passenger might make a few bucks.

Now some will claim that such a law is unnecessary because passengers are independently able to sue. But how often does a passenger sue for lost time. If there is injury, sure. But never for inconvenience.

Any driver, when in an accident with a transit vehicle, must present his or her insurance card to the transit supervisor. But, what if that driver also was required by law to present the insurance card to each passenger? Wouldn't it be more likely that a passenger would claim harm from inconvenience?

Such a law may be illegal or outside the legal scope of a local government, but image the effect on drivers if 60 passengers could also place a claim against the driver's insurance. Wouldn't such drivers be more careful around transit vehicles? Thereby reducing the annual outlay from transit budgets.

6

Employee Owned Transit?

Currently, most transit agencies are run from the top down. The Mayor (San Francisco) or the Governor (Oregon) appoints the transit agency's governing Board of Directors. All policy, hiring and firing, wages, mid-level management structure, and disciplinary matters are decided by the Board or the CEO. Other than union protection, the employees of transit agencies have very little to say about how the system is run.

Just for fun, imagine turning this system on its head. What if (for just a year's experiment) transit employees were allowed to run the transit agency? How would that agency perform and look differently than it does today? If the change were good, would we allow it to continue after the first year?

For such a plan to work, wages would have to be pegged to some objective measure, perhaps the total number of rider boardings per day. That is, by encouraging more people to ride transit more often, the owner-employees would be paid more. However all the owner-employees would divide up a single pool of wage money. This would discourage adding personnel to solve problems unless added employees were actually needed to increase ridership.

For such a plan to work, a fixed operating budget would have to be granted. The new organization could only spend more to operate the system if more income was generated. So perhaps parking meter enforcement would improve, or perhaps more riders would produce more income, or perhaps a federal or state grant would provide more income. All increases in income could only be used for wages if, and only if, the daily ridership increased and then only by that incremental amount. Otherwise added income would have to be applied to operations, improvements, and maintenance.

On the down side, their overall pay would be reduced for each accident wherever the transit agency was at fault.

How would the owner-employees operate under constraints such as these, which would inspire by the promise of increased pay for increased ridership, and would be penalized for accidents that could cost the City millions?

To begin this new setup, would the current CEO be fired or retained as an advisor.

Owner-employees would be made up of all employees, full time, part time, management and union, each entitled to one vote.

The first thing this new organization would be required to do would be to elect its own Board of Directors.

The first thing the new Board of Directors would have to do is hire, promote or appoint a new top management head.

With this new structure in place, what would the riding public see?

1. At first, chaos might follow as the new organization worked the

bugs out its own new internal structure. Would such chaos last a few days or weeks? Would the chaos be visible to the public or merely behind the scenes chaos?

2.   An operator that causes an accident would no longer be immune from punishment and dismissal. After all, if an accident reduces everyone's pay, the owner-employees would likely be less tolerant of such accidents. The public would therefore expect to experience fewer accidents.

3.   A rider's complaint to a driver about a broken door or a late bus or a bad smell would be listened to. After all, the owner-employee has a stake in keeping the rider happy and coming back.

4.   A driver loses money for each rider that boards without paying a fare, so the typical driver would be less tolerant of such fare evaders.

5.   Riders are attracted to vehicles that are clean, quiet, smooth, frequent, fast, affordable, and uncrowded. Would an owner-employee-run agency be more likely to implement stop reduction to increase route speed than the current agency? Would they be more willing to keep

vehicles clean? Would they be less tolerant of cars blocking the bus right of way?

6.   Would parking enforcement start ticketing cars double parked blocking a bus lane? If they did, buses would run faster and potentially draw more riders and thereby increase the wages for the parking enforcement owner-employees.

This may be a pie in the sky exercise, but is worth considering. If a system is not working, every alterative should be included in any discussion of how to fix it.

Maybe Just The Board

Instead of inverting the system to be employee run, perhaps consider restructuring the Board Of Directors to better represent the actual stake holders.

1.   25% should be appointed by the Mayor or Governor as it is now.

2.   25% should be appointed by the district's legislative body (a city council or a county board of supervisors).

3.   25% should be elected from, and by, the employees.

4.   25% should be elected from, and by, the general riding public.

The present Boards are occupied by appointments made by one person. Just how representative is that?

However representation by the public is just as risky. Someone could run on a platform of destroying public transit and win.

This proposal is intended as a basis of discussion only, not as the definitive solution.

7

Who Should Pay?

A minority of citizens believe that public transit should be fully paid for only by those who ride it. Most of those people also believe their gas tax pays fully for new roads, maintenance of existing roads, emergency equipment and personnel.

But in actuality, the gas tax has not increased for over twenty years. The current gas tax only covers a small portion of the cost of maintaining roads for cars. And each year it doesn't rise, gas tax provide less and less money for roads and their associated costs, and the "general" budget provides more.

The U.S. government pays, via grants, a large share of the cost of roads. Although the U.S. government supports roads, it does less for bicycles, walking and public transit.

Even when local governments help pay for the costs of roads, they pay far less in support of walking, bicycling and public transit. People walking require fewer square feet of space compared to cars. The same is true for bicycle. A bus carrying 20 people takes up less room on the road than the equivalent number of cars.

We believe that public transit, bicycle routes, and passengers should receive the same percentage of available funds.

1. The cost of roads are mostly paid by the general public through taxes. So public transit should receive an equal amount.

2. Should the general public also pay for wide sidewalks, and safe signals and cross walks that are safe?

3. Should the general public pay for bike lanes, bike traffic signals, and bike lanes separated from traffic?

4. Should the general public pay for inter-city rail and/or for high speed rail?

5. Should the general public near navigable water pay for ferry service.

In a well structured city or town, each form of transport should share equally from the pool of money allocated for personnel, equipment, capital construction, and ongoing maintenance. Consider that when each dollar of taxes is spent on transportation, each dollar is divided into balanced expenditures:

1. 20 cents is spent on construction, resurfacing, signs, traffic control, and enforcement of motor vehicles.

This includes replacement of overpasses as they age, and bridges as they age. This includes periodic resurfacing of roadways, and resurfacing after utility changes. This includes periodic cleaning of the road surfaces. This includes construction and maintenance of refueling and recharging stations. This includes creation and maintenance of parking lots and structures.

2. 20 cents is spent on public transit, capital purchase of buses and rail, road modification, station construction, drivers, and maintenance.

This includes periodic replacement of mobile equipment. This includes creation and maintenance of stations and bus stops. This includes the special requirements of Bus Rapid Transit, Local Trolly Service, Light Rail and wider service. This includes the construction and maintenance of bridges, tunnels, and separate roads or rails to run public transit apart from traffic.

3. 20 cent is spent on pedestrian safety and mobility.

This includes widening sidewalks, installation and maintenance of crosswalks and signals. This includes modification to roadways to make pedestrians safer, such as speed reduction, and customized crossing signals. This also includes trash removal, snow removal, sidewalk replacement when tree roots make it unsafe, installation of trees for pedestrian shade, and adding safety rails to stairs. It also includes modification of intersections to make them disabled friendly.

4. 20 cents is spent on bicycle safety
    and security.

This includes the creation of bike lanes on existing roadways, and the construction and maintenance of bikeways separate from roadways. This includes creation of bikeways physically separated from motor vehicle roads (such ad by moving parked cars to separate the bikes from traffic). This includes secure parking of bikes off sidewalk, such as indoor bike parking structures.

5. 20 cents is spent on inter-city
    electrified rail, such as light rail
    trains connecting towns together
    at higher speeds than could bus
    rapid transit or express buses.

This includes the construction of elevated sections, bridges and tunnels as needed to separate motor vehicle traffic from inter-city rail. This includes capital laying of rail, the electric infrastructure, and the creation and maintenance of stations. It includes the ongoing expenders of personnel, and other business costs.

High Speed Rail is not part of this division of funds, because HSR is generally funded by state and interstate bonds and private investment.

Most cities and towns divide tax dollars differently. One common division is: 80% for number 1 (motor vehicle), 10% for number 2 (public transit), and 10% for all of rest (3 pedestrians, 4 bicycles, and 5 intercity rail).

Lane County, Oregon spends: 60% for number 1 (motor vehicles) 25% for public transit (a separate funding source) 10% for number 3 (pedestrians) and

5% for number 4 (bicycles) and 0% for number 5 (intercity rail).

A better division would be to legislate equality between number 1 (motor vehicle support) and number 2 (public transit). And to reserve no less than 20% of the pie for the others (pedestrians, bicycles, and intercity rail).

Another approach would be to join public transit with intercity rail under the umbrella of a new state office of Public Transport or Department of Rail Transport, and grant it a slowly growing division between itself and motor vehicle support.

8

Traditional Funding

Current public transit is funded using one, or several, of the sources outlined below. We hope that state legislators will see possibilities for future funding by reviewing this list. We list them below and expand on them in the balance of this chapter.

1. Traditional Taxes And Fees

    - Sales taxes or Value Added Taxes
    - Property taxes
    - Private contract or purchase of services.
    - Lease Revenues
    - Vehicle Fees (title, registration, tags, inspections, smog tests)
    - Advertising Revenue
    - Concession Sales Revenue

2. Business and Related Sources

    - Employer payroll taxes
    - Vehicle rental and lease fees
    - Parking Fees and overtime parking penalties

- Realty transfer tax and mortgage recording taxes.
- Corporate Franchise Taxes
- Room Occupancy Taxes
- Business License Fees
- Utility Fees And Taxes
- Income Taxes
- Donations
- Other Business Taxes

3. Revenue Derived From Projects

- Transit Oriented Development and Joint Development
- Value Capture
- Beneficiary Charges
- Special Assessment Districts
- Community Improvement Districts
- Community Facilities Districts
- Impact Fees
- Tax Increment Financing Districts
- Right Of Way Leasing

4. User and Market Sources

- Tool Roads and/or Bridges
- Congestion Pricing
- Emission Fees
- VMT (Vehicle Miles Travelled) Fees

Traditional Taxes And Fees

Sales taxes or value added taxes are generally regressive taxes—having a greater impact on the poor than on the rich. It is possible to structure a sales tax that is not regressive, but such taxes are rare. Any state than can enact a non-regressive sales tax, will become of great value to the public.

Value added taxes are mostly of use to the European countries. Only one state has enacted a value added tax (VAT), and that is Michigan.

The San Francisco Bay Area uses sales tax to provide continuous funding for public transit and inter-city rail. Oregon, on the other hand, has never implemented a sales tax.

Property tax is another source of funding for public transit. Such sources are more likely to succeed outside of California (Proposition 13 severely limits property tax in California). In general, increases in property tax require approval by public vote no matter the state.

Private contracts or **purchase of services** are the ways transit district can derive income from public transit assets. For example being paid by an event to provide extra bus service to and from that event. Such events are usually annual, so they represent a weak and infrequent source of funds.

Lease Revenues are derived from the leasing of property and equipment to others. For example, a transit district may own the property upon which they plan to build a new bus hub. The unused land surrounding that new hub could be developed and leased to businesses for new restaurants and stores.

Vehicle Fees (title, registration, tags, inspections, and smog checks) can be a source of revenue for public transit districts. Many states collect these fees at the state level, and may be unwilling to share such income. Other states collect these fees at the county level, and may be more willing to share these funds with public transit.

Advertising Revenue is derived from posting advertising on the inside and outside of public transit vehicles and stations. Advertising Revenue can also derived from advertising wraps applied to the outside surface of vehicles, or applied to the pillars and floor of public transit stations. Some transit districts find this form of advertising can cover almost 20% of annual costs.

Concession Sales yield revenue from the sale of souvenirs and snacks. This category includes the profit from installing vending machines on public transit property. If snacks are prohibited on public transit vehicles, then the usefulness of such vending machines are limited. But if eating snacks is permitted on public transit vehicles, vending machines could become a good source of revenue, and might possibly exceed the added cost of cleaning.

Business and Related Sources

Employer payroll taxes used to fund public transit are usually based on the number of employees, and the assumption that employees are the most likely to ride public transit. This is the preferred funding source for the Lane Transit District in Oregon.

One effect of such funding is that it discourages the adding of more employees, because this tax amplifies the cost of each employee.

Vehicle rental and lease fees are derived from a public transit district renting or leasing a bus, van, or other support vehicle to a third party. For example, leasing a fleet of vans to a non-profit to haul the elderly and disabled to a public transit stop, or directly to their destinations.

Parking fees and overtime parking fines can also fund public transit. In order to implement such a source outside of the San Francisco Bay Area, some state laws would have to change. For example, in Oregon state law prohibits public transit from deriving income from managing parking and parking enforcement.

Realty transfer tax and mortgage recording taxes are fees that can be increased in support of public transit. Again this may have to be supported at the state or county level. Such fees could be applied to all mortgage events, or merely to commercial property events.

Corporate Franchise Taxes are taxes not based on corporate income, but on a per corporation basis. For example, the tax may be based on net worth or capital held by the corporation. A franchise tax essentially taxes corporation for the privilege of doing business in the state.

Room/Occupancy Taxes (also known as a hotel tax) is a sales tax on the money charged by hotels and lodging houses for stays of 30 days or fewer. Because it is based on short stays, it is a tax paid mostly by visitors, rather than residents. Because it is based on a fixed percentage, this tax tends to be regressive.

Business License Fees are fees charged to issue, or renew, a business license. Such fees must be minor to encourage the creation of new businesses. In a large city, such fees may be collected on a regular basis. In a medium to small town, such fees cannot be relied upon on any regular basis.

Utility Fees And Taxes are collected for rubbish pickup, gas for heating and cooking, electricity, and network connectivity, including phone service. Because such fees and taxes can usually be collected on a monthly basis, they are attractive as a source of funding for public transit. Such taxes and fees can be regressive, or if well designed, progressive.

Income Taxes are not collected by all states. Those that do collect income taxes, usually earmark such revenue for the general budget. The legislative branch would have to pass laws to reserve part of such taxes for public transit.

Donations are funds given to pubic transit by the wealthy, foundations, or corporations. Donations are more likely when a transit district is a non-profit tax deductible organization. Most transit districts, however, are government run.

Other Business Taxes are things like inventory taxes, property tax, and excise tax. State legislators would have to enact other sorts of business taxes, perhaps as a public transit business tax.

Revenue Derived From Projects

Transit Oriented Development and Joint Development projects are generally large projects such as building a multi-story residence near a light rail stop. If the public transit agency co-financed a building, the public transit district could share in the profit from collecting rent. Or a public transit district could build a bridge over a river for its buses, and collect tolls from private vehicle that also used that bridge.

Value Capture secures and recovers a portion of the benefit delivered by public transit, in order to offset the cost of the investment itself. The degree that public transit adds value to the private sector can be recovered by taxing that increase. For example, in San Francisco new business high-rises are taxed based on the square footage added. The assumption is that a large fraction of those working in that new building will get to work on public transit.

Beneficiary Charges are the costs of a fund transfer that a third party pays. Such things as wire transfers, direct deposits, financial to financial company fund transfers. The person paying for the transfer can be taxed a small amount per transfer in support of public transit.

Special Assessment Districts work by adding (assessing) an additional tax on top of the existing property or sales taxes for funding pubic transit. The specific form of assessment district that is useful for public transit is a "Transportation Improvement District." Such districts are zones in which additional taxes are captured from property owners to fund improvements to the area. Specifically improvements to public transit that add value to the district.

Community improvement districts are areas of non-residential properties, whose owners choose to pay an additional tax or fee to benefit public transit, because improved public transit will benefit the area.

Community facilities districts are special taxation districts (usually a separate political subdivision. Property taxes are usually assessed to finance, acquire, construct, and operate public transit in the defined area. Such districts are usually associated with rebuilding a formerly blighted area. The disadvantage is that residents of the district are taxed more than those outside the district.

Impact Fees are fees imposed on a new or proposed development project to pay for all or a portion of the cost of providing or extending public transit to the development. Impact fees can be based on the cost of construction, or some metric related to that construction. Such fees are often fiercely opposed by developers.

Tax Increment Financing Districts create special tax districts around targeted redevelopment areas from which future tax revenues are diverted to finance infrastructure improvements and/or development. For example, if a new shopping center is being developed, future tax revenue from that shopping center could be used in advance to finance improvements in public transit that would benefit that shopping center.

Right Of Way Leasing can produce income for the transit district. For example if a railroad wishes to install rail over part of a transit district's property, the transit district could lease that property instead of deeding it. Such leases could supply a transit district with a reliable monthly income.

User and Market Sources

Toll Roads and/or Bridges can become a source of income for a transit district. For example, a transit district heavily improves a highway for Bus Rapid Transit, it should be allowed to collect tolls on the improved stretch to offset its construction costs.

Congestion Pricing is a method to reduce the car crowding in a busy area by charging each vehicle a fee to access that area. In addition to the goal of reducing car crowding, congestion pricing can also provide and income for public transit.

Emission Fees are fees charged for undesirable emissions, such as smog, and carbon dioxide. For example, a city might want to discourage gasoline powered cars and may do so by charging emission fees. Clearly it would benefit public transit if such fees were used to finance it.

VMT (Vehicle Miles Travelled) Fees are being proposed to offset the drop in effectiveness of the Gas Tax. As vehicles become more fuel efficient, and electric cars slowly replace gasoline cars, a shift in taxation will become mandatory. At that time, this new tax should be computed to both support highway construction and maintenance, as well as to support improved public transit.

Summary

In this chapter we have illustrated and explained a wide array of possible sources of revenue for public transit. No methods are suitable for all transit districts, but a sub-selection might prove valuable to some.

Part 3

The Transit Rider

"Walking is the only form of transportation in which a man proceeds erect - like a man - on his own legs, under his own power. There is immense satisfaction in that."

— Edward Abby, Postcards from Ed: Dispatches and Salvos from an American Iconoclast

9

Customer Is Always Wrong

Imagine growing up in a town were a bus can be boarded using any door. Now visit a town were the rule is to board only at the front. What happens if you enter through a back door? Yes, that's right, the driver yells at you and orders you to get off and enter through the front door.

The customer on public transit is the transit rider. Most businesses bend over backward to insure that customers have a pleasant experience and want the customer to return. But that is not so within public transit.

1. A woman is kicked off a bus because the bus driver does not believe her service dog is an official "service dog."

2. A elderly man is kicked off a bus to make room for a wheelchair.

3. A person with all door boarding, visits a city with front door only boarding. That person is yelled at when boarding through the rear door.

4. A fare inspector stops every person from exiting to check tickets and passes. If a fare was unpaid the fair inspector issues a ticket for non-payment. Fare inspectors are almost always demanding and rude.

These are only a few of the complaints voiced about bad treatment on public transit. Most transit districts treat the transit rider more like the enemy, rather than like a valued customer.

No store would evert treat customers so poorly. Consider the hypothetical business equivalents of the above numbered complaints

1. A restaurant refuses entry to a blind person with a guide dog because they don't allow dogs.

2. A hotel elevator operator tells an old man to take the stairs, because two people in wheelchairs are waiting to board.

3. A man is asked if he parked in the parking lot. When he says, "No. I took the bus." He is told he needs to enter through the front mall entrance on the other side of the building instead.

4. An usher in a movie theater demands to see your movie ticket and writes you a $100 dollar fine if you cannot produce it.

A well run transit district must strive to attract customers by continuously improving service and through hiring cheerful and caring personnel. Everyone from the drivers, to ticket sellers, to management and fair inspection, must treat transit riders as customers or friends, and not as the enemy.

10

Transit Rider's Bill Of Rights

The transit rider must be guaranteed certain rights held in common by all transit providers. Just as transit providers may restrict activities such as smoking and eating, they must also guarantee a common set of rights shared by all riders (customers).

What follows is one suggestion for such a Transit Rider's Bill Of Rights:

1. The public transit rider shall be defined as anyone who requires or desires access to public transportation for mobility. The public transit rider is not limited to the poor and elderly. It shall be defined as including all people, whether or not they currently use public transportation for mobility.

2. The public transit rider must never be required to wait more than 15 minutes (one quarter hour) for the next public transit

vehicle for the selected route to arrive. This is similar to the maximum amount of time a driver will circle a parking lot waiting for a parking place to become available. Fifteen minutes is universally the maximum time any reasonable person should be expected to wait for anything.

3. The public transit rider must have access to public transit 24 hours per day and 7 days per week. A town would never close streets, bridges or sidewalks at night. So why should a transportation district shut down at night? A town would never routinely reduce the number of lanes on a major road on Sunday, nor should public transit service be reduced on Sunday.

4. The public transit rider must never be required to walk a distance greater than 1/8th mile (201 meters or roughly two football fields lengthwise) to access a transit stop. Imagine that garages were forbidden. How far would a driver be willing to walk to access his or her automobile? As a corollary, if an 1/8th mile circle were drawn around every transit stop in a system, there should be no area without access.

5. The public transit rider must not be required to pay extra to transfer from one route to another. It is impossible for one route to uniformly cover and entire city. When there are multiple routes, some riders require the ability to transfer. Barriers to free transfer shall be prohibited.

6. The public transit rider must never be prohibited from boarding a public transit vehicle because of race, age, religion, nationality, gender, health, physical ability, or sexual orientation. Bicycles must be accommodated except when they adversely effect passenger access, boarding, or safety.

7. The public transit rider must never have health or safety threatened, and at all times must be protected from harm. This includes safety when approaching a transit stop. Such protections, might be: never having to cross a busy street to reach transport; never needing to run to catch infrequent transport; and never being warned about a sudden stop.

8. The public transit rider must be provided with clean, comfortable transport. No public transit

vehicle shall become soiled,
littered, or defaced in such a way
as to cause transit rider
discomfort or fear.

9. There shall be no difference in
rights between public controlled,
owned, or operated transit and
privately controlled, owned, or
operated transit.

10. No transit rider shall be subjected
to offensive language or
threatening behavior because of
transit district policy.

11. The transit rider may sue a
transit agency for redress should
any of these rights be abridged
without sound reason.

These rights are suggestions only. Depending on the specific country, region, or city policies, they may be required to be weaker or stronger. But at a minimum, Every transit district should declare the rights they are affording the traveling public. And the riding public should be encouraged to push back against any limitation of those rights.

11

Mission Street Body Count

Imagine typically warm autumn day on San Francisco's Mission Street, where it crosses 16th street. A steady flow of automobile traffic travels both directions on Mission street, mixed with the occasional MUNI bus. People arrive by BART's subway to fill the sidewalks. Many folks also shop among Mission Street's many stores and restaurants.

Now float above mission street using google maps or any other tool at your disposal, and notice the use of the "street-space," the area between buildings on either side of Mission Street.

Sidewalks are nearest building fronts, parking spaces on both sides of the street are next, and two lanes of traffic in each direction complete the picture. Exclude bus stops, and this is the pattern all along Mission Street from 16th Street to 17th Street, a distance of one-tenth mile or 528 feet.

Because the average width of a sidewalk is 8 feet, a parking place is 7 feet wide, and a traffic lane is 10 feet wide, the total area between the buildings on each side of Mission Street between 16th and 17th Streets is roughly 36,960 square feet. The below table of "Square feet by mode of transport" shows how that total is divided based on the current modes of transport.

Table 1: Square feet by mode of transport

Pedestrian	23%	8,448 sq. ft.
Parking	20%	7,392 sq.ft.
Traffic	57%	21,120 sq. ft.

Assume the average parking space is 17 feet long. That length would allow 31 cars to park on one side of the street, or 62 total to park on both sides.

Assume that automobiles travel with at least one car length between them. That would allow 20 cars per lane, or 80 total for all four lanes in both directions.

Assume at least half the drivers were not alone in their vehicles. So 40 cars would have carried 40 total people and the other 40 cars would have carried 80 total people for a grand total of 120 people.

Assume the parked cars were also well behaved, so 31 would have carried 31 total people, the other 31 would have carried 62 total people for a grand total of 93 people.

Finally assume that there is one couple (two people walking together) occupying or walking on the side walk each eight linear feet of sidewalk space. From actual experience the sidewalks on Mission Street are more crowded than that, but this estimate provides a fair lower guess. In 528 feet of each sidewalk, that would mean 132 pedestrians on each side or 264 total.

Table 2, below, shows the share of square feet based on persons.

Table 2: Square feet per person

What	People	% of sq. ft.	square feet	% people	Should get sq. ft.
Peds	264	23%	8448	54%	19958
Park	93	20%	7392	21%	7761
Car	120	57%	21120	25%	9240

Note that, when the share of square footage is calculated based on the number of people transported, pedestrians (54%) of the people, should be entitled to the lion's share of square footage.

In terms of the square footage between the buildings (in our example case that was 36,960 square feet) one is persuaded to ask how a single car compares to a single person?

A typical full-sized car is 16.5 feet long and 6 feet wide, or 99 square feet. A typical pedestrian can occupy a square yard comfortably, or 9 square feet.

This begs the question: Why should one person in a 99 square foot automobile have more right to use that 99 square feet than would the 11 people that could comfortably occupy that same space. In other words, why does automobile ownership grant the right to more square footage than is the general right of every individual to that same public space?

In general, more people drive in the city than probably should. They drive because driving is more convenient, less time consuming, and more comfortable than public transit. Driving has achieved this level of convenience because so much of the city's real estate has been given over to driving. In addition to driving lanes and parking lanes, many sidewalks are crossed by driveways that lead into and out of parking lots.

If driving is a privilege, not a right, why does that privilege so often trump the right to walk?

We should invert this relationship. Streets should be designed primarily for pedestrian use and only for automobile use when low pedestrian density allows.

For example, when resurfacing a street, or when defacing a street due to subsurface work (such as replacing sewers), take a moment to examine the pedestrian load. If sidewalks are crowded because of high pedestrian density, use that crowding as a mandate to redefine the area. Eliminate a driving or parking lane or both to restore the balance. Naturally in low pedestrian density areas, it may be possible to reduce the size of a sidewalk to add parking. A formula, regulation, or law should be devised that forces recomputing of "street" area whenever the street undergoes construction or reconstruction.

Next time you go for a walk, pay attention to the traffic in the street next to you. How many cars contain a single driver without passengers? How much space does each lone driver get compared to the size of your sidewalk? Ask yourself, why does that single driver have more rights to our common space than you do?

Another way to view the answer to this question is as a speed limit. Instead of reducing the number of lanes of traffic, instead reduce the speed limit and allow pedestrians to share the road with cars.

For example, instead of increasing the width of the sidewalk, instead reduce the speed limit to a speed that is safe around pedestrians. Perhaps 5 m.p.h.

At that speed pedestrians could safely dart between cars to cross the street. Or when a movie lets out, the crowd of pedestrians could overflow into the street with much reduced risk.

In this example, the reduced speed of 5 m.p.h is a suggestion. Perhaps a slower speed might be better.

Because drivers would doubtlessly complain of such slow speeds, the alternative of widening the sidewalk might be preferred.

Part 4

Planning

"If you fail to plan, you are planning to fail."

—Benjamin Franklin

12

If An Elevator

Imagine what a city would be like if elevators were run by public transit. You enter the high-rise where your office, or doctor, or lawyer is located. and find, instead of a button to push, a display showing how many minutes you have to wait for the elevator to arrive. The sign, by the elevator, shows 30 seconds to the next elevator, over and over for the next five minutes. Or at least that's how long you may be willing to wait before taking the stairwell up.

On days you wait for the elevator to arrive, the door eventually opens. You would step on, but people trying to get off the elevator are being blocked by too many people trying to get on. Pushing your way past a shopping basket, you find a place to stand with a strap hanging from the ceiling.

Too late, after the elevator started, you realize you got on a limited that will not stop on your floor. You decide to stay on anyway and just walk down one level using stairs. But today's elevator is slow because too many people want to ride, so it takes a full minute to board everyone at each floor.

You are delayed again on the 30th floor because the elevator door on that floor had been manufactured too high so steps had to be used to get into and out of the elevator. This delay had been caused because a wheelchair required that a special ramp be laid down so that the disabled could board.

You almost make it to your floor when two elevator inspectors get on and demand to see everyone's elevator pass. You wouldn't mind, but you have always found the elevator inspector's a bit pushy.

You get off just as a local elevator going down arrives. You board it, rather than walking down one level using the stairwell. You finally arrive on your floor after a twenty minute ride up 29 floors then down one.

Public Transit As An Elevator

Imagine if a transit vehicle was run like an elevator. Every bus stop would have a transit-card reader installed next to, or under the transit stop structure. By tagging your card you would automatically notify the next arriving bus you wish to board. If a bus stop served multiple lines, a button on the card reader could be used to specify the route sought. Tagging ahead of time would minimize the number of riders that would need to tag while boarding and thus speed up boarding.

As a corollary, a ticket machine should also be present at every bus stop. Or at least at stops routinely troubled by too many cash boarders.

When the bus arrived, all doors would open so that those disembarking would not unnecessarily delay those boarding.

All buses, and all trolleys (when present) would have elevated stop platforms so that all boarding is done using platform that is level with the bus/trolly floor. This not only speeds up wheelchair boarding, but also speeds up stroller, shopping cart, and rolling luggage boarding. As well as speeding up boarding for the infirm, elderly, or injured who find steps troublesome.

In Closing

Next time you take an elevator, compare that ride to your most recent Public Transit ride and wonder, as we did, why Public Transit cannot favorably compare.

13

Grid Versus Hub

For reasons that are difficult to fathom, most transit districts prefer the hub approach over a grid approach. The hub approach is designed to cause every route to begin at the hub and proceed out from the hub and returns along the same route back to the hub. To reach anywhere other than the hub, requires a trip inward to the hub and then another trip outward from the hub. The distance for any trip from point A to point B becomes the sum of the distances from A to the hub plus the distance from the hub to B.

The Hub Approach

Consider, for example, the minimal hub design shown in the figure on the next page:

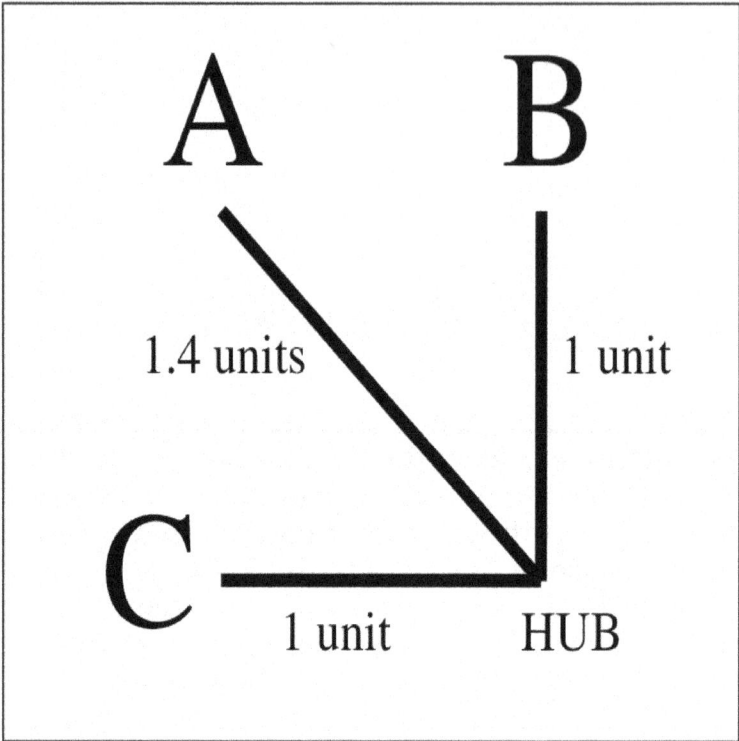

In it, three routes service all four points and the total distance for all possible trips are:

A...B = 2.4

B...A = 2.4

A...C = 2.4

C...A = 2.4

B...C = 2

C...B = 2

A...hub = 1.4

hub...A = 1.4

B...hub = 1

hub...B = 1

C...hub = 1

hub...C = 1

==================

total   20.4

If the route from B to the hub is out due to storm damage, there will be no way to reach point B from anywhere else on the network of routes. That is, until the damage is repaired, or until a detour can be established for the route. Because of this design fault with a hub, the transit rider is always out of luck.

The Grid Approach

An alternative to the hub approach is called the grid approach. The grid may require a transfer to reach another destination. The grid approach is more immune to route outages but requires 1/3 more vehicles to run, or the same number of vehicles running with lower frequency than the hub approach.

The minimal grid is shown on the next page.

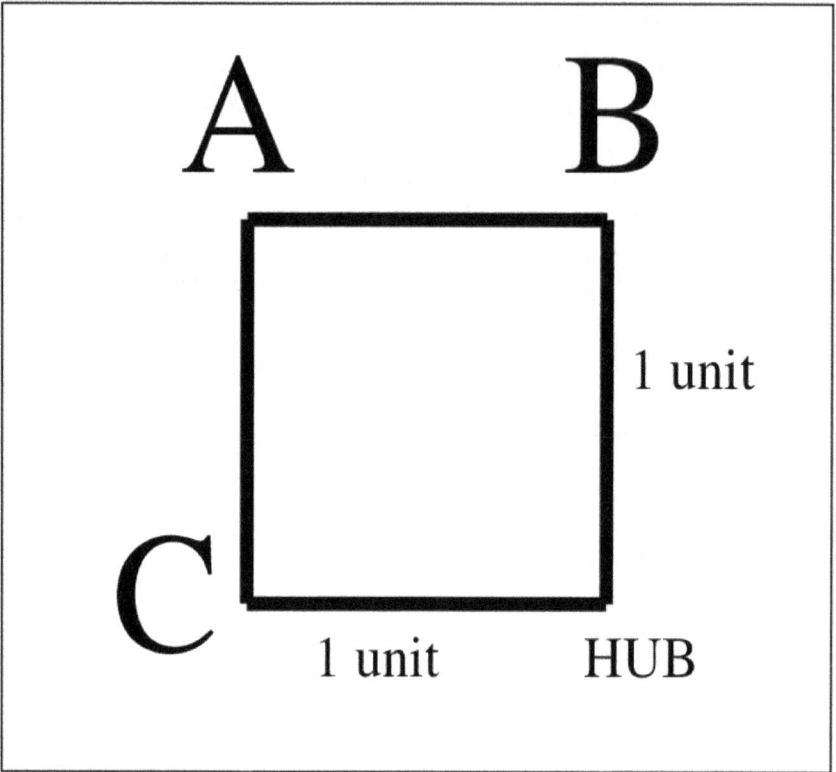

In the above figure, four routes service all four points and the total distances for all possible routes are:

A...B = 1

B...A = 1

A...C = 1

C...A = 1

B...C = 2

C...B = 2

A...hub = 2

hub...A = 2

B...hub = 1

hub...B = 1

C...hub = 1

hub...C = 1

==================

total   16.0

If the route from B to the hub is out due to storm damage, you can still get to hub by traveling from B to C, or from to B to A, and then to the hub. Sure this is a trip of distance 3, but that is certainly better than waiting for hours for a down route to return to service.

Note that the total distance of all possible routes is less with the grid approach

hub total 20.4

grid total 16.0

The minimal hub approach uses three vehicles to travel 20.4 units or 6.8 units per vehicle. The grid approach uses 4 vehicles to travel 16 units or 4 units per vehicle. That means the grid vehicles can travel 21% more often than the corresponding hub vehicles, thereby reducing the cost of the extra vehicle.

Finally note that the hub approach presumes that everyone needs to come to the hub. The grid approach makes no such assumptions. With the grid approach, route intersections become the dominant feature. Because half the destinations will require a transfer, timing of arrivals at transfer points becomes crucial.

The High Speed Belt

A variation on both the grid and hub approaches is to add one or more high speed loops around the center. Because of the high speed required, such loops are more expensive to construct than are the internal bus, or BRT, or trolley lines. A loop, for example, must have no grade crossings and must logically have two tracks with vehicles traveling both directions around the loop at once.

Consider the abbreviated illustration below:

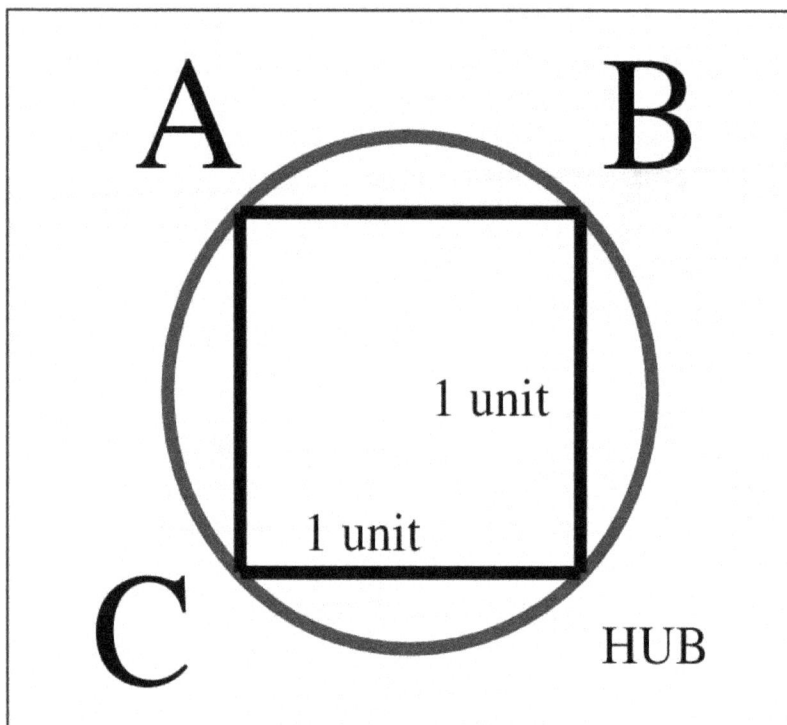

In the above figure the regular line vehicles travel at 1 unit per hour and the loop travels at an average of 5 times that speed. So now one has a choice. For a trip from A to the hub, one can go on route A to B and transfer, and then take route B to the hub. That trip takes 2 units of time. Or the rider can take the belt loop (shown in black circle) from A to the hub in 1/5th the time or 0.4 units of time.

We grant that a belt line makes little sense in a micro route as in our examples, but consider its advantage to a fully developed grid system as shown on the below. Sure it is small when compared to actual transit district maps, but it serves to illustrate the advantage of a high speed belt line.

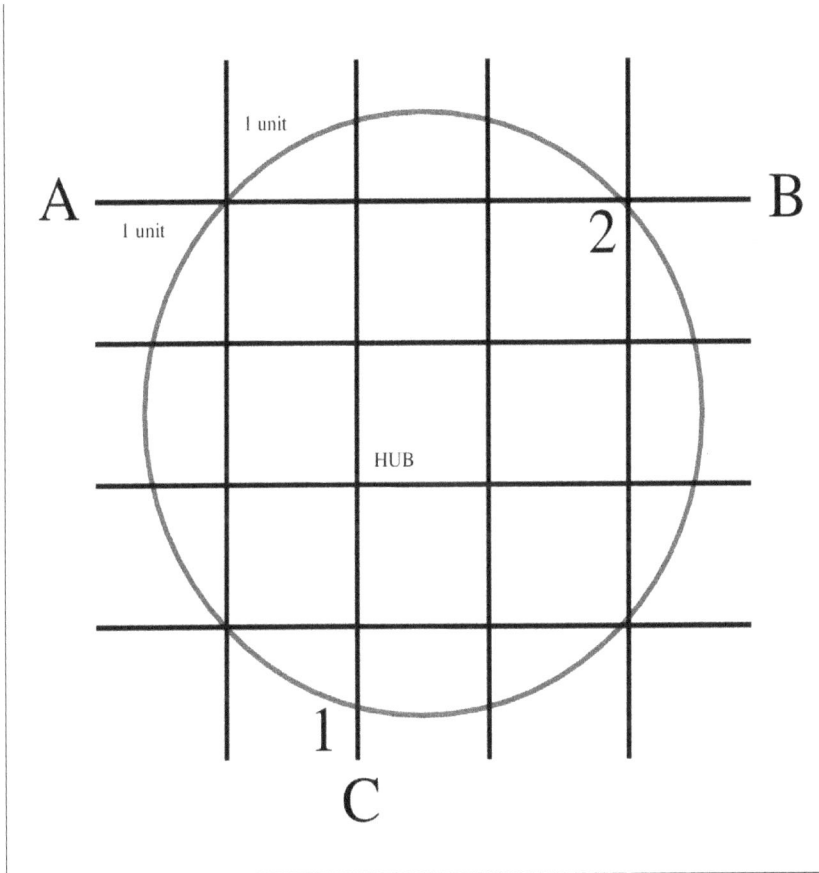

Now consider a trip from C to B. The normal route would be to travel vertically up the C line to the A/B line, transfer and then travel horizontally to B. That trip is 7 units with one transfer or 7 units of time. With the belt-line the trip is faster but requires two transfers. The traveler takes a bus up on C 1/2 unit to the belt-line. There the traveler rides at 5 time the speed over 5 units or from points 1 to 2. And then a transfer to route A/B and a bus trip to end at point B for a total of 2.5 units of time. Clearly the belt can improve trip times on many start to end trips, including those inside the loop.

Consider a trip from the hub to end point B. The bus route would take the traveler up the C line two units to route A/B. The traveler would then transfer and travel 3 units right to end point B. That is a tip of 5 units distance or 5 units of time. Next consider the trip from the hub down to point 1, there to catch the belt-line from 1 to 2, and thereafter to transfer to the A/B line and travel 1 unit to B. This latter trip would require only 3.5 units of time.

Note that a 5x belt-line greatly benefits the hub approach. It gives the travel more choices and, in most instances, can reduce trip times.

In Conclusion

To compare and contrast the hub versus grid approaches, consider:

- The grid is more adaptable to route outages then the hub.
- The grid makes no assumptions about departure or arrival destinations.
- The grid allows the traveler to chose the preferred route.
- The grid encourages timed transfers to minimize transfer wait times.
- The grid works even better when a 5x or faster belt-line is installed.
- The grid approach uses 1.4x to 2x more routes then the hub approach, but the grid's routes tend to be 42% shorter routes.

14

Multi-Dimensional Plans

Most transit designers examine the problem of idealized transit using a two-dimensional graphics. This makes sense, because most cities are laid out flat like on a map. Placement of bus stops then becomes a simple geometry problem. How do you arrange bus stops so that no place in the city is further than 200 yards (meters) from a bus/transit stop? Simple isn't it?

Yes, but there are variations on that theme. Should, for example, the distance from stops be drawn as circles or squares or diamonds or stars? But no matter the variation, the assumption of two-dimensions remains consistent.

Many cities has hills, and some have fairly steep hills. One way to represent steep hills on a flat map is by drawing streets further apart when they are steep. Another method is to color the steep parts more red and the flat parts more green. Unfortunately neither approach supplies the correct information. Buses use more energy and travel slower up steep hills, but use less energy and can travel faster down hill. Passengers can walk downhill far easier to a bus stop than uphill to one.

- A third-dimension might make the problem easier to model. If each intersection on the map also had that intersection's altitude.

83

- The greater the positive (uphill) steepness between two intersections, the worse for uphill bound buses, and the worse for passengers to walk uphill to a bus stop.

Another factor that is absent from the two dimensional model is the popularity (demand) at each intersection:

- Two lines crossing create a transfer intersection (multiple crossings lines increase demand).
- Population density surrounding a stop increases demand.
- Shopping density surrounding a stop increases demand.
- Office density surrounding an intersection increases commute (episodic) demand.
- Event venues surrounding an intersection increase episodic demand.
- Elderly specific venues increase demand for nearby and/or downhill access to transit stops.
- Schools increase demand.

Another factor is the likelihood that an intersection will bar or slow transport.

- Part of a parade or celebration route closure requires nearby access to alternative transit stops.
- Common point of failure (shared overhead wire for example) can disable two or more lines at once (increased risk).
- A bus turning in traffic should be penalized because of speed loss.
- High traffic density at an intersection slows (penalizes) buses.
- Political protests unpredictably slow transit.

- Intersections with a significantly higher than average accident rate should be less likely to be located on transit routes
- Wide busy streets slow pedestrian access to a stop across the street.
- Long traffic signal cycle time with no bus override should penalize the intersection
- Lack of a bus only lane should penalize an intersection.

As you can see, many considerations must go into a transit system design. One way to model the information is as a (possibly multi-dimensional) graph, another is by using a database. Which ever method is chosen, all the above considerations should probably be included in it.

Given complete information, a program could be written that would lay out the optimum transit system for any city. Has such a computer program been written? Has such an approach ever been used for a large city ore even a small city?

It is time to bring public transit design into the 21st century.

15

The A/B Plan

Some cities plan to speed up bus routes on selected corridors by eliminating every other stop. Thus far, few changes have been made to reduce stops using this technique mostly because of public outcry against such stop eliminations.

Here I propose a simple alternative to stop elimination that inconveniences few and speeds up bus travel for all. I call this plan, bus leapfrogging, or odd/even stops, or more simply A/B stops. Consider:

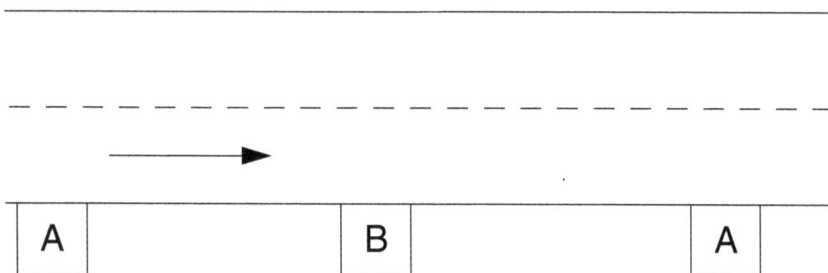

| A | | B | | A |

A bus line is running in the direction indicated by the above arrow. Pretend this is a major commute line. The line-A bus would only stop at A bus stops. The next following bus (the line-B bus) would only stop at B bus stops. In this manner both the line-A line and the line-B line will run faster than the former every stop line did, thereby reducing the number of buses needed to service that corridor, and providing swifter transit for all.

For such a scheme to work, several details may need to be considered and built into the plan.

- Both lines must stop at major transfer intersections. For example, both line-A and line-B must stop at the transfer intersection.
- In no circumstance should the distance between any A and any next B stop be further than a normal city block.
- In no circumstance should access to the other line require travel up hill or up stairs.

Cost Of An Experiment

An experimental route could be set up to judge the effect. Paper signs could be used during the experiment. The public would have to be surveyed to judge the public success of the experiment. Bus drivers would need minimal training.

Advantages

- It is well known that stop elimination can speed up a route. It therefore follows that this A/B plan will also speed up a route.
- Stops appear eliminated, but no stop are actually eliminated.
- A problem solved with signs and training is better than a problem solved by removing physical stops.

Disadvantages

- This is not a good solution on low frequency lines. Doubling the time to wait at any given stop hurts the typical rider when that wait interval is longer than 15 minutes.

- At night, and other times ridership drops and the interval between buses increase, those less frequent buses could become AB busses, e.g. the line-A + line-B, or a line-local which makes all stops.

16

All Door Tagging

All door boarding benefits a transit district by allowing passengers to board or exit by any door. This reduces dwell time* at stops. If the only people to board at the front are those that pay cash, access to all doors will reduce boarding time.

Of course all door boarding requires the means to check for fairs paid at all doors (assuming public transit is not free). Generally such fair checking is made using transit cards (like London's Oyster card, Seattle's Orca card, or San Francisco Bay Area's Clipper Card). Armed with such a card, one needs only tap (or tag) a card against a card reader to pay the required fare, or to board for free.

Use of cards and card readers has several advantages:

1. A card can be filled with funds using a web interface or with machines at a major transit center.

---

*. The amount of time a bus stays stopped a a bus stop.

2. A card can hold a monthly pass, such as an adult, student, senior, or disabled pass.

3. A rider can board transit without having to carry the correct change, or any cash at all

4. If a card is lost or stolen, it can be canceled and quickly replaced.

Transit cards can also aid in transfers. Some transit systems allow a paid fare to continue for a fixed interval. In San Francisco, for example, once tagged on, a card will not be charged again, even if tagged-on again within the grace period of 90 minutes.

Another approach would be to see if the time from a tag-off and the time of the next tag-on is within an expected layover interval for transferring. For example, when one tags-off at the hub and ten minutes later tags-on to the bus to the movies, that second tag-on should not be charged.

Another advantage of tagging is in data collection and behavior analysis. Few transit districts, for example, seem interested in collecting all possible data. By requiring riders to tag on *and* tag off, better tracking of rider behavior becomes possible.

If a disproportionate number of people exit at a minor stop, for example, plans could be made to upgrade that minor stop into a major stop. Or, as another example, if no significant number of riders ever transfers between this line and a transfer line, the nature of the transfer stop might need to be redesigned.

Boarding behavior could also be determined by the address associated by the rider. What if many transit riders lived between two stops and all boarded at one of those stops. Perhaps the other stop is up hill, or lacks a shelter, or is over the tracks, or means walking through a risky neighborhood, or is unlit at night. Such information could help redesign the offending stop or eliminate the offending stop.

Tag cards (and more recently tag phone software) hold within them a simple concept, the means the transit district to easily and more fully understand the behavior of its riders.

If the billing address of the transit card owner is known, more relevant information becomes useful:

- If the person is not local, the use of a particular transit stop can indicate the neighborhood in which the visitor is staying.

- If the person is local, the distance between the person's home and all nearby bus stops will be known. For all local riders in that same neighborhood the most useful transit stops can be computed.

- When riders tag on and off each ride, the transit district can compute the number of riders that take one form of transit and then transfer to another form (as from a bus to light rail, or from a bus to a subway).

- If a large number of riders live in a neighborhood that is under served by local transit, new transit lines can be proposed and developed.

- If too many riders live in a district that is served by a bus line, the transit district could propose and develop a light rail line to replace it.

The more data the transit district has available to it, the better job it can do to provide constantly improving service.

17

Level Entry

Most buses are elevated so that people boarding must climb two or three steps to enter. Most buses are equipped with ramps that can be lowered for folks with wheel chairs (to chose just one example). Others that pay to ride must wait for the wheel chair to roll aboard before they can board and pay.

Most buses can carry bicycles (often at most two at once) on bicycle racks attached to the front of the bus. Mounting a bicycle on that rack can take a minute or three. Similarly, when disembarking, it takes a minute or three to lift the bike off and to raise the rack.

In addition to wheel chairs and bicycles, buses also create friction:

- People with foot or leg injuries, sometimes using crutches, can have trouble using stairs.
- Pregnant women and women with babies, often need to roll a stroller aboard. Such people are inconvenienced by bus stairs.
- The elderly and infirm often have difficulties with bus stairs.
- Travels pulling rolling luggage may have trouble lifting a heavy suitcase up steps.

- People with small dogs sometime travel with rolling pet carriers. Hauling those up and down stairs can be difficult.

- Small children sometime have difficulty going up and down stairs.

All of these problems can be solved by creation of level entry, where the boarding platform is level with the entry floor of the transit vehicle. Generally, the two edges of those surfaces must be close enough to eliminate a dangerous gap*.

In San Francisco, for example, light rail has long boarding stations in the subway and at stations south of Market Street. Those long stations platforms allow level boarding for all doors. But only a few stops north, west, and east of Market Street have level boarding only at the front door. The remaining stops do not allow level boarding.

In Eugene, Oregon, for example, Bus Rapid Transit vehicles (called EMX for EMerald eXpress) provide all door level boarding. The rest of the non-EMX buses require the rider to mount stairs, except at the front door, where a ramp can be extended to the sidewalk.

In the ideal world, all public transit vehicles would have level boarding for all doors. It is too bad we live in an imperfect world.

---

*. Hence the British, "Mind The Gap."

18

Good For the Goose

Parking meters in many cities are not enforced between the hours of 6:00 p.m. through 6 a.m. which means from early evening through the following early morning. The effect of this non-enforcement is that cars may park for free during those hours.

In addition, many parking meters are not enforced on Sundays. Again this allows cars to park free all day Sundays.

Businesses: Many businesses claim that periods of free parking are vital for them to run a successful business. If those hours were reduced, they claim, their businesses will be harmed.

Residents: Many residents claim to require overnight free parking because they lack private garage parking. They too claim they will be harmed if those hours of free parking are reduced.

Public Transit: Riders of public transit claim to be harmed every time fares are increased, and every time service is reduced. Riders of public transit are never

allowed to ride for free except possibly for
New Years Eve.

What is good for the goose is good for the gander.
In all fairness, if cars can park free during certain
hours, then public transit should run for free during
those same hours.

- Why should someone have to squeeze between
  two cars, that are parked for free, in order to
  pay to board a bus?
- Why should someone be late because a paid
  bus ride is delayed because a car ahead of the
  bus is parallel parking into a free parking
  space?
- Why should someone pay for a bus ride to a
  store, when that same person could drive to the
  same store and park for free?

Why not make everyone happy and make everything free from 6:00 p.m. until 6:00 a.m every day?
That is, free for both public transit and parking.

After all, fair is fair. And what is good for the
goose (parking) is also good for the gander (public transit).

19

On Demand Public Transit

The problem with normal public transit is that it was never designed to properly support three sorts of customers.

1.   Suburbs have always been designed to discourage easy access to their insides. Because of their low population density, there is no reason to run buses through such difficult to access neighborhoods.

2.   The disabled often find public transit stops too far away, or the stop nearest their destination is too far away from their destination. Such people need public transit, but find normal public transit too inconvenient to use.

3.   The sick and elderly often find public transit stops too distant, or that destination stops are not near enough to doctors and hospitals. The sick and elderly

need public transit but find
normal public transit too
inconvenient to use.

In cities like San Francisco, Seattle, Chicago, and New York, the disabled, sick and elderly have access to taxies and ride shares. Also those mature cities lack modern difficult to access suburbs.

In many smaller cities, however, the city core is surrounded by suburbs. The need for On Demand Public Transit is most evident in such smaller cities.

Lane Transit District

The Lane Transit District (LTD) is centered around the combined metropolises of Eugene and Springfield in Oregon. Support for On Demand Public Transit is provided by RideSource, a fleet of vans that are ADA compliant. Unlike public transit, same day service is not provided instead the rider must a arrange for a ride no later than 5:00 p.m. the day before.

Once you are registered with the service, a van will pick you up at your home and will drop you off in front of your destination. The rides are free.

People registered with the Oregon Health Plan can also use RideSource. But they may have to pay for mileage, or their trips may be free.

To register for RideSource, you phone a local number and request an interview. Someone will visit your home for an in-depth interview. After the interview it takes up to 20 days to decide your case.

Valley Transit Authority

The Valley Transit Authority (VTA) covers San Jose, California. Support for On Demand Public Transit is called Paratransit and includes a fleet of ADA compliant cutaways, minivans, sedans and taxis. The rider must register with VTA, undergo a phone interview, and, if accepted, that rider is issued an ID card.

Normal trips must be arranged prior to 5:00 p.m. the previous day. Normal trips are $4.00 each.

Same day trips, second vehicles, extended service area, or open return trips. Such trips are considered Premium and cost $16.00 per trip. Such costs are additive, so a same day trip with an open return would cost $32.00.

Modified Public Transit

The below diagram shows one way that normal public transit can be modified to adapt On Demand service.

The normal bus is traveling up to stop first at A and then at B. But imagine if a phone app could cause the bus to turn right to pick up a rider at C. The bus would have to return to its normal route so that stop B is not skipped.

The obvious flaw in this design is that the main route from A to B and further up will produce ill will when detoured occasionally to C.

Skipping Stops

Another means to solve these problems is to use smart bus stops. Such stops can be constructed closer together and there can be more of them.

Smart bus stops work best when several bus lines overlap. For example if the A5, A6, and A7 bus lines all share the same stretch (say a mile) of a road, they could benefit from smart bus stops.

A rider arrives at such a bus stop and is given a choice of three bus lines. If the rider select bus line A6, then only the A6 bus will stop there. The other two lines will not stop there.

A bus rider tags onto a bus, and is given the choice of which stop he or she wants to exit. Either the rider types in the number of the stop, or the rider is shown a map of stops and touches the stop on the map. In either instance, the bus will stop at that indicated bus stop. Armed with advance knowledge, the bus driver will not have to watch each stop to know if a rider is waiting. Bus travel will be faster even when there are more bus stops.

The disadvantage, of course, is the child effect (such as a child pushing all the buttons on an elevator). A child, or a childlike adult, might push all the buttons of a bus stop, causing all bus lines to stop despite nobody waiting. Or selecting multiple stops after tagging on, causing the bus to stop and many unnecessary stops.

Another scheme could utilize a smart phone. A bus district's app could not only allow you to tag on with it, but tagging on could also automatically select your exit stop. That same app could also notify the bus driver at which stop you are waiting.

None of this tag or button or app approach is simple. It would require careful design, complex software design, hardware design, bus retrofits, and the construction of smart bus stops.

Perhaps a transit district should perform an experiment and implement such a scheme on a single line to test if it actually improves transit performance.

Part 5

Long Term Planning

"It is more often referred to as a long-term plan. Do you know what you want your program to look like in the next five years? ten years? Start now!"

—John Benham *Music Advocacy: Moving from survival to Vision.*

20

The Oregon Rail Project

Rather than spending hundreds of million of dollars exclusively on expanding freeways and freeway interchanges, the state of Oregon should consider a more sustainable carbon free alternative.

One such alternative is to connect all the cities of the state with electrified rail. This doesn't have to be high speed rail, because anything significantly faster than driving will lure people out of their cars. A class 7 track would work wonderfully, because trains could run up to 120 miles per hour. This is not high speed rail that achieves speeds over 250 miles per hour, but more affordable medium speed rail. The idea is to allow travel from any city or town in Oregon to any other city or town in Oregon in significantly less time than driving.

The state of Oregon already plans to spend millions of dollars to upgrade the track along the Amtrak corridor so that diesel trains can travel faster. However these trains must still share tracks with freight trains. And these existing diesel trains risk collision by crossing many streets. When a train crosses a street, that is called a "grade crossing." Automatic arms lower to stop traffic, but that can still risk a vehicle becoming stuck on the tracks, or people accidentally walking across the tracks to be hit. This becomes even a more likely scenario when trains travel at 120 m.p.h.

A state rail project could lay class 7 track along a private right of way, by building bridges or tunneling where necessary to avoid grade crossings. That right of way must be for the exclusive use of passenger travel, and would bar access to fright trains.

Passenger trains could however haul baggage, mail, small packages, and other light freight in common with passengers. For example Fedex might want to purchase one or more electrically driven cars to be hauled along with passenger rail. There would have to be weight limits, otherwise bridges would become too expensive to build.

Although electrified track is twice as expensive per mile to construct than diesel track, it is also environmentally better. Electrified trains are lighter than diesel trains, so bridges may be built for a lighter load.

After 50 to 75 years of construction, the entire system might be complete,

How should such a large system be paid for and constructed? Two sources make sense:

1. A statewide non-regressive sales tax. Perhaps only on related purchase such as gasoline, diesel, tires, car repairs, batteries, and parking. Or perhaps on all potentially unhealthy items, such as carbonated drinks, alcohol, and pot. Or perhaps on all these and more.

2. Toll roads. Perhaps turn all on-ramps to interstate freeways into toll booths. Or perhaps toll on all parking places using property tax measures. Or perhaps a toll when automobile registration is renewed, based on miles driven.

It is not the purpose of this essay to recommend any form of rail construction funding over any other form. Only elected representatives could make this decision.

When envisioning this rail network, other than city centers stations, what other stations might be desirable? Other such centers that could require stations might be:

1. Airports. Every airport that serves the public with regularly scheduled flights might host a rail station in close proximity to the airport's entry.

2. Population centers. Not all population centers are in the middle of a town or city. Often the actual peak of population is in some neighborhood well away from the city center. Such additional population centers might also be served by a rail station in addition to the downtown.

3. Universities and Colleges. Centers for learning can be large enough to be considered a unique population center. Such centers for learning might also be better served by rail stations.

4. Some may believe that commercial venues should also have train stations. Such venues as shopping centers or fair grounds my seem desirable, but perhaps might be better served by local trolleys or buses?

Intra-State Freight

It might make sense to run rail freight to many of the same locations as passenger rail. The state might determine that instead of running two tracks of passenger service, it would make sense to run four tracks, two for passenger service, and two for freight.

Because freight is generally heavier than passenger cars, bridges and elevated sections of track will have to be constructed significantly stronger. Four tracks make the system more resilient, because a derailing on the freight line could allows freight on a section of passenger tract to bypass the outage. Similarly a derailing on the passenger line could allow passenger trains on a section of freight track to bypass the outage.

For such a dual system to work, both passenger and freight would need to be identically electrified, with the same gauge and class of track.

21

A Fictional Example

The SFMTA stands for the San Francisco Metropolitan Transportation Association. The SFMTA is sometimes called MUNI by local San Francisco residents. The furthest ahead that the SFMTA now looks is a mere two years ahead. Their official vision for two years hence is:

> "Providing timely, convenient, safe and environmentally friendly transportation alternatives... SFMTA enhances the quality of life of San Francisco."

Such a weak and shortsighted vision is not worthy of the respect of the San Francisco public.

That City deserves a great deal more than this watered down sentiment. At the very least the SFMTA should develop a ten year plan and even better would be a thirty or fifty year plan. Devise a vision of what public transport should look like in the future and make that vision so damned exciting that the public can't help but support it. The figure on the next page offers a glimpse of what San Francisco's rail transport should look like twenty-five years hence.

Noriega/Beach Geary/30th

Sunset/Judah Balboa Cliff House

Lake Merced 24th/Judah

Zoo Vicente 28th Ave 19th Ave Polo Fields

SF State/Stonestown 14th/Lawton Slow Lake Geary/10th

H-Loop **G-Loop**

Stern Grove 14th Ave Museums Geary/7th Seacliff

Portola 7th Ave USF Calif/Presidio

Woodside UCSF Fell Alamo Sq

Belt-Loop Monterey Oak/Divisidero Presidio **F-Loop**

Haight/Ashbury Chestnut

Geneva/Mission **D-Loop** Clipper

Dolores Park 16th/Valencia Calif/VanNess Broadway/VanNess Bay St

Silver Calif/Filmore Broadway

Van Ness/Market Lombard

E-Loop Civic Center **C-Loop** Chinatown North Beach Pier 39

Cezar Chavez 22nd St Church/Market Union Square Embarcadero

Cortland/SanJose Castro/Market Powell/Market Montgomery

B-Loop

Silver 16th/Valencia 12th/mission Moscone/Mission

24th/Valencia

Candlestick Cezar Chavez Portola Pottrero/22nd Folson/10th Moscone/Howard

A-Loop Caltrain Main/Bryant

Evans Marin 16th UC SF

Transbay Terminal Ferry Building Fishermans Wharf Ft. Mason Palace of Fine Arts

Hunters Point ATT Park

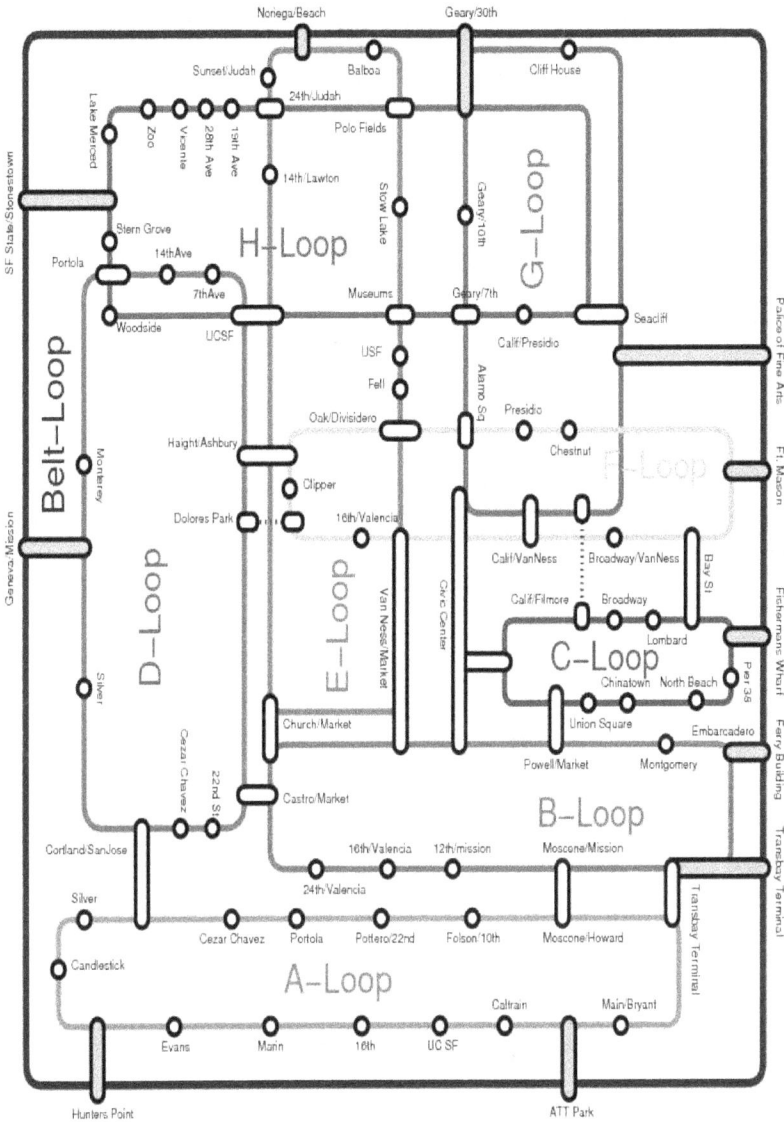

A high speed rail circles around the edge of the
city and many internal somewhat slower internal
underground loops connect to that outer circle for easy
transfer to a much faster line. A plan like this is a pipe

dream perhaps, but illustrates one way to plan for the future.

To illustrate one of SFMTA's shortcomings, consider the Central Subway plan. A subway connecting the Third Street T-line to Chinatown. The SFMTA has presented this plan as the conclusion (phase 2) of the "Third Street Light Rail Project." Questions have been raised about the value of such an expensive project, which terminates in Chinatown instead of continuing (as it should) into North Beach and Fisherman's Wharf. Imagine how much easier this subway, or any other subway, would be sell to the public if the SFMTA had already created a vision for a new and truly exciting future. Instead of the Central Subway finishing a project, it could have been just the next small part of a network of future envisioned subways.

It is far better to dazzle the public with a grandiose vision, than it is to sell the public over and over again with a sequence of seemingly disconnected projects.

About The Author

Bryan Costales is an American Author born Chicago, Illinois and raised in Concord, California. His vocations have ranged from news photographer, to window designer, to display manager, to art director for motion pictures, to Unix system administrator, to software engineer. His writing career began with a modest technical book called "C from A to Z." Since then he has written several technical books culminating in "sendmail" (the bat book) for O'Reilly Media. He has professionally published several short stories. He studied with the San Francisco Writing Salon, the San Francisco Writer's Grotto, and the Grape Writing Method. This book is his fifth technical book.

Bryan currently lives in the Great Northwest with his lovely wife Terry and his nimble dog Gypsy who cannot yet jump through a hoop. Among other things, Bryan currently dabbles in are photography and gardening.